walls        have        fallen
at           the         margins
a            place            for
o             a               k
thrown                    ashore
by           the             sea
the        descent          into
root-ways              leaves
and      water    knots    of
grey      rope     they     are
a      d      r      i      f      t

# FIELD  NOTES
*( Volume  One )*

*Corbel Stone Press* publishes
audio recordings, texts, art &
photography.

*Proprietors*

Autumn Richardson
Richard Skelton

*Printed Publications*

Typography of the Shore
Skin & Heather
Induviæ
Into the Bare Moorland
Wolf Notes
Field Notes (Volume One)

Corbel Stone Press
Cumbria, UK.
www.corbelstonepress.com

*Field Notes (Volume One)*

Published on the 20th of March,
2012, by Corbel Stone Press.

ISBN 978-0-9572121-0-7

First Edition.

Printed in the UK on recycled
paper.

This book gathers together four out-of-print titles from the *Field Notes* series – a loose-fitting collection of *place-poems,* each originally published as a limited edition, handsewn chapbook.

Within the series itself there is considerable variety in scope and form – from single poems to small collections; from abstract collages to observational studies; some the result of a single encounter, and others the fruit of several visits, over a period of months.

To these we add a new, previously unpublished collection, *The Flowering Rock,* written during our time living upon the west coast of Ireland throughout the spring, summer and early autumn of 2010.

It is our hope that, as the series develops, it will become a poetic map of seemingly disparate locations – a distillation of what is unique to each, whilst also charting the underlying connections that may exist between them.

*Typography of the Shore*

*A. Richardson & R. Skelton*
Tentsmuir, Scotland
20th December, 2008

shell casts in sand

empty presses

birds track salt lines in
tidal measures

*footnotes*

*addenda*

*marginal scrawl*

bracketed between
strand and drift

struck through

by sea

at the margins of the sea
behind the drag of tide
fetched up – departed

*heaped broken reeds*

*vertebral dregs*

*clotted feathers*

*bladderwrack and*

*driftwood strands*

*shards of mussel*

*glass and wire*

*skull of small bird –*

*spine still clinging*

*light limned around*

*orphan pools*

revenants

on the fossil shore

*desiccated*

*remaindered*

*stricken*

*bleached*

*exposed*

*prone*

*etched*

*brittle*

*hallowed*

*fleeting*

*forgotten*

ragged shoreline
spurred stems ascending
brome and fescue
wind-kerned grasses

*matted*

*threshed*

*bridled*

*thefted*

*winnowed*

*burnished*

and in the surface of the water
a corresponding shirr

for every hare's tail

its answer

infaunal creatures
ebb-drawn to
ferine surfaces

become the
carrion of
sands

*Skin & Heather*

*R. Skelton*
Anglezarke, England
2005–2008

a threshold

a moment of transition

climb the small stile

gather the small stream

leaves and water

the constant polyphony

moors like scar tissue




skin and heather

ghosts of buildings

families of shadows

a fissure

a feather

a gradual surrender

to stones, dirt and grasses

receive the river

its sudden lulls

without weight

or consequence

forming

binding

dismantling

everything you ever knew

*Induviæ*

*A. Richardson*
St. Helen's Wood, England
September–November, 2008

*The unattended stones        the tumbled
walls        a path sickled through grasses.*

i. A forgotten field

Skeletal rays of hogweed,
dried blood of sorrel,
earthnut,
yarrow –

marrrowless husks;
lushness pared down
to vegetal bones.

The remains of umbellifers.

Desiccated stems / withered leaves.

Seed-heads bend beneath winds.
Stands of fireweed chafe to a shine
in the sun's last light –

a field of corpses
they sway, rise, sigh;

The wind through panicles, coarse-throated;
cough of burr, achene, through nightshade, yarrow.

ætheric imprints still hovering,
flesh departed,

roots still pumping,
hoarding light
into the cellaring cold.

Frayed / bowed / swept / mown.

Sitting in the leaf-litter
I watch
antennæ hunt through
the undergrowth
drift through loam
erupt from the inner
ridgings of bark.

Seeking, dowsing, foraging.

iii. Wood notes, October 18th, 2008

Saprotrophs bloom
bloodless from
the skins of others;
they harrow
a mouldering bole
(supine now
heartwood cored
flesh for ants and
larvæ).

Constellating bark and deadfall.

Birch saplings crowd
the understorey
lean into green pockets of light
leech with weed-vigour
from the nourishing dead.

v. Into November

I sense the downward cycling,
the saps' decline,

the descent into root-ways,
tuber-ways.

The waning. Leaves mould into loam,
fold over seeds and roots.

The sky sags round-bellied with rain.

The stream-bed swells;
waters bruise through ribs of soil,

cough up leaves of oak and
beech, torn stalks of bracken,
wind-culled branches.

Winter rains / winds. Disarticulations / sloughings.

The wax of life recedes, curls into rest.

Caches drip-feed roots, seeds, shoots;
blood in the dens of the slumbering.

The wood rests
(*sloughed frayed torn*).

A hold for the fallen
(*secretly vital*).

*Into the Bare Moorland*

*R. Skelton*
The West Pennine Moors, England
May, 2010

into the bare moorland
unhindered
nature will remake
again

let the moorland
go to bracken
and others
will follow

furze and broom
they come after bracken
thriving
to make a richer soil

furze will reach outwards
dying at its heart
and into its remnants
rowan and birch will seed

they are edge trees
and in time will make
a place for oak and
ash and pine

let the moorland
go to bracken
*and others*
*will follow*

*The Flowering Rock*

*A. Richardson & R. Skelton*
Ballyconry, County Clare, Ireland
March–September, 2010

*From the water*      *they rise and fall*
*blue hills breathing*      *songs without words.*

Each morning
and the sounds of birds,

of wind
and water.

Each morning
and the ever-changing hues of the sea –

its manifold greys,
browns, greens and blues.

Down on the shattered rocks,

madder
and thrift

eyebright
and hart's-tongue –

blooming minutiæ.

The scars hold life,

are living seams of green,
amber, cerulean, rose.

Spring gentian,
     *ceadharlach bealtaine;*

blackthorn,
     *draighean* (wretched one; penetrator);

sea spleenwort,
     *fionncha mara;*

bitter vetch,
     *corra meille* (crane's pea);

cowslip,
     *bainne bó bleachtáin* (milk of the milch cow);

herb robert,
     *eireaball rí* (train of the king);

wild garlic,
     *gairleóg;*

primrose,
     *sabhaircín* (delight, pleasure);

dog violet,
     *fanaigse* (fragile weed);

early-purple orchid,
     *magairlín meidhreach.*

The walls have vacancies,
interstices, vents —
they seem a pale net-work;
knots of grey rope
staked out to land
the great catch.

Those weir-men who
stitched them, laid them,
have long gone, down
within the hills' pores,
but whether by luck
or design the walls
stand still, whilst haw
and rowan heave and sigh,
catching the wind's
ceaseless expirations.

Listen.
A low, muted,
bell-like sound.

They are *na clocha clingeacha* –
the ringing stones –
the bell stones.

Tread lightly.
Remember their voices
amongst the rocks.

First

the hooked mouth
of the sea

second

the drill
of the water

third

the bleat
of the heather

fourth

the dwarf
of the earth

fifth

the head
of the copse

sixth

the cut-throat
of the hedge

seventh

the little singer
of the willow

eighth

the clacker
of the gorse.

As the sea retreats
a way opens

to the blackened rocks
of an ancient and natural corridor.

The oldest, most enduring,
and yet most insubstantial road.

More ancient than bohreens,
than green roads, drove roads.

Commuted by heron, oystercatcher
and snipe. Forested by sea-oak.

Carpeted by red and green
and brown.

And beyond the shore

*ghost islets*
                emerge,
        glimmer briefly,

then resubmerge –
revenants
of the waves.

Avens, thorn, fern
prostrate juniper
fold into fissures
harbour within stone

and beneath

arterial passages
underground flows
wailing notes
of water and wind

the hollow songs
of hollow hills.

blue          grey          violet


                fissured        scarred          eroded


fluted          caved          porous


                rill-worn      costal          yielding

Along the shattered pavement
are *scailps* (clefts, fissures, grikes) –
joints and seams prised open
over millennia –
the tireless work of water
(of acids and gravity)
as it flows
towards the
resurgent
stream.

An old way
has turned to greening

returned to bloodwort
crane's-bill
and meadowsweet

ending in a hazel wood
thickening over forgotten fields.

Here grey walls have fallen

succumbed to roots and
the steady perambulations of rain

to hawthorn and bramble
winding through heartstones.

Elders bloom
throughout the aged garden

(planted by hands for fever
for breathing through a long winter)

and nettles
have reclaimed the hearth.

The medicine remains
(needing neither roads nor hands)
engulfing the traces left

returning furrow and field
to wild meadow and woodland.

Milkwort,
  *lus an bhainne;*

silverweed,
  *briosclán* (brittle one);

hawthorn,
  *sceach gheal* (white haw);

sea campion,
  *coireán mara;*

bloody crane's-bill,
  *crobh dearg* (red talon);

sea pink,
  *rabhán;*

sanicle,
  *bodán coille;*

common butterwort,
  *bodán meascáin;*

wild strawberry,
  *sú talún fiáin;*

wall rue,
  *luibh na seacht ngábh* (herb of the seven gifts).

Through narrow rooms,
along the small lengths
of stone corridors, passages, precincts

     *birds*     *glimmer*

alight on jutting tongues of stone
(from the open
mouths of rock fissures)
find resting chambers,
a moment's pause,
a brief dimming.

Pulled along
unseen, familiar lines,
the bird glides
heavily
with rigid, graceless wings.

Eventually it will ground,
this grey, silent kite.

It cannot endure on memory
and repulsion alone.

This shy bird is *corr réisc,*
the marsh bill,
but it could equally be called
*an dealbh srutha,*
the river statue,
or *an chloch a stánann,*
the gaze stone –
crouching, motionless,
on the furthest reaches of the boat cove.

But sometimes
it breaks its vow of silence –
a premonitory, piercing cry.

And then truly it earns the name
*corr scréachóg,*
or screech heron.

And further up the shore,
a white kestrel
hovers over the waters.
*Seabhac mara.*
A watcher of forms
beneath the blue-green
glass. A sudden diver
into the shifting tide.

Time after time
it makes a knot in the sky,
holding the fury
of the air at bay
with slow wing beats,
waiting
for a glint
of silver below.

The physic garden. Four centuries derelict.

*Rosemary*

*feverfew*

*vervain*

*dog-rose*

*wormwood*

*ramsons*

*mint*

flourish still. The elder has seeded a small wood.

Seeking a desert
they came to these blue stones.

Seeking desolation
they found instead the flowering rock.

Devil's-bit scabious,
    *odhrach bhallach;*

bird's-foot trefoil,
    *crobh éin* (bird talon);

yarrow,
    *athair thalún* (ground father);

carline thistle,
    *feochadáin mín* (fine thistle);

wall lettuce,
    *leitís bhalla;*

wood sage,
    *iúr sléibhe* (mountain yew);

selfheal,
    *duán ceannchosach;*

wild thyme,
    *tím chreige;*

lady's bedstraw,
    *boladh cnis* (the scent of skin);

harebell,
    *méaracán gorm* (blue thimble).

There is a clamour
down by the sea.

Gulls congregate
on the narrow islets
just beyond the promontory.

Common,
black-headed,
lesser black-backed,
greater black-backed.

And mingled in
with the laridæn chatter –
the fraught piping of the curlew,
and the plaintive, solitary
calling of the oystercatcher.

Do they sense the downward cycle too?
The turn away from the sun.
The descent into autumn.

*Muich,*
> sadness, dullness; a mist, a fog;

*murchortha,*
> things thrown ashore by the sea;

*murdhuach,*
> a mermaid, a sea-nymph;

*murdhubhchaill,*
> a cormorant (black sea hag);

*murgabhal,*
> an arm of the sea;

*murmar,*
> a murmur, noise of talk or of the sea;

*murse,*
> sea-shore, sea-marsh;

*murthol,*
> tide, flowing of the sea;

*murthoradh,*
> produce of the sea;

*toichim,*
> going, departing.

From the water
they are adrift

blue hills, dark with rain.

What the stones enfold
remains their own.

What the tide pulls away
returns transformed

if it returns at all.

If the liver has a sound
it will be this sound –

the drag and suck of waves

waters filtering through weed
through sand

tirelessly, tirelessly
swabbing shore-stones

turning grit to glass.

*Notes*

Ascender, the upward projecting stem of a lowercase letter, such as '*b*' or '*d*'.

Brome, a grass of the species *Bromus*.

Cast, the mould used to make metal type.

Ferine, wild, feral.

Fescue, a species of tufted grass.

Hare's tail, a coastal species of grass.

Infaunal, dwelling within sediment.

Kern, the action of adjusting the spacing between pairs of letterforms.

Measure, a means of determining proportions; also, *metre,* or units of rhythm in poetry.

Press, i.e. *letterpress,* the means of marking a page with metal or wooden type.

Ragged, unjustified type; a region of type in which one margin is kept unaligned.

Shirr, drawn together; a gather in the texture of a fabric.

Spur, a serif-like ending to the stroke of a letterform.

Stem, the main, usually vertical, stroke of a letterform.

Strike through, to delete by means of a straight line through a word.

Tail, the descending, often ornamental, stroke of a letterform.

Tracking, the action of adjusting the spacing between letters and words.

Skin & Heather

*Skin & Heather* is collaged from *Landings* – a book about the West Pennine Moors of northern England.

Induviæ

Disarticulation, to become disjointed, esp. the bones of a body or the stems of a plant.

Induviæ, the withered leaves which cling to the stem of some plants; not falling; remaining for some time.

Panicle, re: grasses: a flower-head which is borne on stalks, which are in turn borne upon branches from the main stem. Also: any branched inflorescence.

Saprotroph, an organism (such as the fungus Sulphur Tuft, *Hypholoma fasciculare*) which derives its nourishment from dead or decaying organic matter.

Umbellifer, of a family of plants, usually aromatic with hollow stems, producing clusters of radiating compound flower-heads, known as umbels. Examples include: angelica, carrot, hogweed, parsley, hemlock and chervil.

*Into the Bare Moorland* was written in absentia, in
Ireland, after reading a passage from *The Permaculture
Way* by Graham Bell.

## The Flowering Rock

Corr réisc, the common Irish name for the grey heron,
which translates as *marsh bill*. Both *river statue* and
*gaze stone* are coinages – many thanks to Caoimhín
MacGiolla Léith, as elsewhere in this collection, for
translating them into Irish.

Corr scréachóg, screech heron, is curiously enough
a folk-name for the screech or barn owl, found in
Dinneen's dictionary, which also mentions *corr scréacha*,
*corr scréadóige* and simply *scréachóg*. Here *corr scréachóg*
has been reappropriated for the heron.

Laridæn, from *laridæ*, the gull family.

Muich, etc, Irish words gathered from the dictionaries of
O'Reilly and Dinneen.

Physic garden, part of a monastic garden used for
growing medicinal herbs. This poem was written after
visiting the ruins of Corcomroe Abbey, a Cistercian
monastery in coastal County Clare.

White kestrel, this, and *seabhac mara* (sea hawk) are
coinages for an unknown bird of the gull family, seen
fishing just off the shore by Ballyconry.

*Texts*

THE PERMACULTURE WAY,
    Graham Bell, 2004.

THE GAELIC NAMES OF PLANTS,
    John Cameron, 1883.

A THESAURUS OF BIRD NAMES,
    Michel Desfayes, 1998.

FOCLÓIR GAEDHILGE AGUS BÉARLA,
    Patrick S. Dinneen, 1927.

IRISH TREES,
    Niall Mac Coitir, 2003.

THE BURREN, A COMPANION TO THE WILDFLOWERS OF AN
IRISH LIMESTONE WILDERNESS,
    E. Charles Nelson & Wendy Walsh, 1997.

WILD PLANTS OF THE BURREN AND THE ARAN ISLANDS,
    Charles Nelson, 2008.

AN IRISH-ENGLISH DICTIONARY,
    Edward O'Reilly, 1864.

LANDINGS,
    Richard Skelton, 2009.

*The Field Notes Series*

Typography of the Shore,
A. Richardson & R. Skelton, 2009.

Skin & Heather,
R. Skelton, 2010.

Induviæ,
A. Richardson, 2010.

Into the Bare Moorland,
R. Skelton, 2010.

Wolf Notes,
A. Richardson & R. Skelton, 2011.

The Flowering Rock,
A. Richardson & R. Skelton, 2012.

CORBEL STONE PRESS